Kaleidoscope of Life

Harriet Rounds

PUBLISH AMERICA

PublishAmerica
Baltimore

First printing

Softcover 9781462696956
PUBLISHED BY PUBLISHAMERICA, LLLP
www.publishamerica.com
Baltimore

Printed in the United States of America

Kaleidoscope of Life

Harriet Rounds

8/1/12

DOROTHY
Pamela's Mother

I know we have only met once or twice
I also know you are very nice

I want to thank you for your gift to me
Even though I know it was given unintentionally

Because of you, I have a tremendous friend
Whom I will cherish until the end

Pamela loves, honors and adores you
I am sure the feelings are mutual too

Most of us are blessed with wonderful mothers
Some are a little more special than others

Pamela is a friend, loyal and true
All qualities I know she got from you

November 7, 2011

THANK YOU, PAMELA

God saw me floundering and said "What can I do
I know, I'll send Pamela to you

She'll care for you and do all she can do
Even make you smile when you are feeling blue

Should you need a hand to hold, she will be there
Should you need a hug, she will do it because she cares

She will wipe away your tears
Console you if you have fears

She will give you shelter on a winter's night
She will do what she can to make things right

She will laugh with you and cry with you
She will do everything that she can possibly do

Pamela is your friend
She will be there to the end

And, of course, if you do something silly like you usually do
She will say "Oh my aching ass, what am I going to do with you?"

A WARM GOODBYE

We just had a chance to say hi
And, now it is time to say goodbye

A task that is difficult to do
Because I am really going to miss you

You have class and you have style
A warm friendly smile

I know you have to do
What's best for you

So with a tear in my eye
Here's a hug and a warm goodbye

A BEAUTIFUL SUMMER DAY

The sky and sea seemed to be one
A beautiful day to sit in the sun

The beach was nice and clean
There were some sights that should not have been seen

The waves gently kissed the shore
And, the seagulls just seemed to soar

I am so glad you called and said "Hey,
Let's go to the beach today."

So many others had the same thought
We were lucky to find a parking spot

Anyone would think it was a summer's day
Or at least the end of May

But, it was October 9th and we sat in the sun
Doing nothing at all, but we sure had fun

7/16/12

A DAY AT THE BEACH

Hundreds of people were on the shore
But, there was still room for lots more

Up against the blue sky
Puffy white clouds drifted by

Sand sculptures were a magnificent work of art
I wouldn't even know where to start

Seagulls were everywhere
Making a racket as they flew through the air

They even stole a man's lunch
I didn't realize they could be such a terrifying bunch

All in all the day was such a delight
I wouldn't mind going back tonight

The water was warm when I stuck in my toes
And, the sun left me with a red nose

The smell of the salt water lingers with me
My favorite place to be has always been near the sea

4/19/12

A GIFT OF FLOWERS

Three men at the store
Bought flowers before they went out the door

The first man said his girl was feeling blue
He thought buying flowers was the thing to do

I smiled and said that's a nice thing to do
Then another man walked by carrying flowers too

I asked anniversary or birthday
He said no, I just decided to say

That I love my special lady
And, we might just have a baby

A third man man ran by and said in case I make a mistake
Some flowers for my lady, I will take

These three men all made me smile
Going shopping that day was worthwhile

1/27/12

A NEED TO WRITE

I have to write today
For whatever reason, I can't say

I've written letters by the dozen
To friends and my cousin

Sometimes I ramble on
From twilight to dawn

There are times when words just tumble out
I can write a poem without hesitation no doubt

There are also times when nothing is there
I don't write and don't seem to care

I like to write letters as well as poetry
Sometimes I think it helps keep my sanity

A SLOWER TIME

Yesterday things moved at a slower pace
No one was in a hurry to win the race

People were very polite
They always said hello or have a good night

There was no rush to get anywhere
And, the people really cared

Men tipped their hats when a lady went by
And, children would smile when you said hi

Children were polite too
Temper tantrums would never do

A total stranger would open the door
They would do all they could for you and more

It's so sad how things have changed
Entire lives have been rearranged

Now people don't even smile at you
They back off as if they fear you too

It is so sad what we've done
A world of uncaring people is what we've become

With all my heart, I hope and pray
That things will slow down one day

7/2/11

A WISH

I've always wished for world peace
I still wish John were not deceased

I wish my kids would be happy
But, I am afraid that is not to be

I wish I would hit the lottery
Alas, that's one wish that will never be

I am not saying I want to be someone's wife
But, it would be nice to have someone to share my life

Someone to hold me near
And, say "I love you, Dear"

I wish there were days I had no pain
Or my body would not hurt so when it was going to rain

In many ways I am luckier than most
I have a home, family and friends from coast to coast

I also have a gift for making words rhyme
So I guess this is just my wishing time

December 27, 2011

A WONDERFUL GIFT

I was lying in my bed
Thoughts of Christmas running through my head

It was quiet and very late
December 24th was the date

Suddenly, I heard a sound
A sound that was so profound

Outside in the dark night
This sound filled me with delight

Suddenly, I was a child again
It brought me back to way back when

I heard the bells on Santa's sleigh
Such a wonderful gift for Christmas Day

10/6/11

AUTOMATED PEOPLE

Everyone walks around without a smile on their face
Makes me wonder what happened to the human race

When people are driving in their car
There minds are someplace else, not where they are

People have all become living robots
They move as if they are automated pilots

They have forgotten life is worthwhile
And, have forgotten how to smile

People no longer know what to do
Unless a machine says "Try it, it's new"

Sometimes I have looked at people and have cried
Close relationships seem to have died

I don't like the way things are being done
Nor do I like the what we have become

Progress is truly great
Give me back people before it's too late

To me, a smile, a hug or a hand to hold
Is worth much more than a pot of gold

3/12/12

BACK THEN

Times were tough back then
But, I wish we had those times again

Daddy was a fisherman out to see
Mommy took care of the family

Looking back, I remember the worry on her face
But, she'd smile and the worry left without a trace

Mom and Dad had it really rough
Sometimes there really wasn't food enough

But, the love in our family made us strong
We always managed to sing a song

Financially we were poor
But, everyone was welcome at the front door

We were rich in other ways
We took pleasure in simple things, back in those days

We took time to smell the flowers
We took walks in April showers

We didn't rush
We had trust

We loved one another
My sister, brothers, my Dad and my Mother

At the end of the day
We would always pray

It was by no means perfect back then,
But, In a heartbeat, I would do it again

BEAUTIFUL BLUE EYES

He said I have beautiful eyes
But, his eyes could definitly hypontize

His eyes are as blue as the sky
Just looking at him and I get high

He leaned over and kissed my cheek
Suddenly, his lips I did seek

Just a quick loving kiss
It was a chance I could not miss

I wish he would hold me and never let go
I have to admit, I love him so

We talked about going away
We always say "Someday"

Someday when the time is right
He will hold me tight

Someday he will look into my eyes
And, he will be totally hypnotized

August 8, 2011

BETTY THE BEAR

Betty sits in her bikini upon my bed
I have to wonder what is going through her head

She has an impish smile on her face
And, Mom would say what a disgrace

Although Betty will never be seen
I think it is kind of keen

She sits on my bed or in a chair
Betty is my favorite teddy bear

BLIZZARD OF '78

Snow flurries were forecast
Just a little storm, it wouldn't last

Three days later, all we could see was white
Snow covered everything in sight

Snowbanks went to the second floor
We were lucky to get out the door

Cars were buried everywhere
If you made it home, you stayed there

I called my Mom on the phone
She lived a half hour away and was all alone

She said the snow is over my window
I don't know what to do, I just don't know

Driving was not allowed for quite a while
But, we went anyhow and made her smile

We cleared away all the snow
Gave her a hug and drove home very slow

We made it home safe and sound
And, prayed we would soon see bare ground

BUSY TIME

It's been a long and busy week
Some answers I still seek

I'm not always sure what to do
Although I try to be like you

I go to work every day
I even remember to pray

From sunup to sundown
I feel as if I am being bounced around

I miss the days when things moved at a slower pace
No one cared who won the race

Whenever I can, I love to watch the clouds drift by
I thank God for all the beauty that catches my eye

6/7/12

CANCER

One 6 letter word causes so much fear
And, it touches everyone we hold dear

Cancer raises its ugly head
Fills everyone of us with dread

It touches young and old
Even animals I am told

The hell, the torture and the pain
Cancer touches everyone and it's insane

So many people have to endure
Pain and grief and I know there is a cure

Granted not everyone can be saved
But, God bless them all, they are brave

May 9, 2011

COLOR CHART

Do you remember the color chart
We had when we took art?

Eight colors is all we had
And, eight colors wasn't so bad

We had red, yellow, green and blue
Orange, brown, black and white too

Now we have seventeen
Shades of green

There are so many hues
Of blues

And, all the different shades of red
Still bounce around in my head

Then Crayola came out with colors numbering 64
And, today they probably have lots more

Who would ever know
We would have more colors than a rainbow?

9/24/2011

COOKIES AND TEA

Cookies and tea
Sounds really good to me

Friends sometimes go for a walk
Or just sit and talk

Sometimes we cry
For someone who said goodbye

Then we laugh over something fun
When we walked around in the sun

We say we should do that
And,.realize we need a hat

That would never do
Not for me or for you

I think it is time for a pick me up
I will make tea and you can use my best cup

Cookies and tea, for you and me
That's how friendships should be

COOKOUT

It's that time of year
When people come from far and near

We found a place in the shade
And, the salads are all made

The grill is giving off lots of heat
Please tell me it is time to eat

There's lots of chips for dipping
Even a rope for skipping

Kids swimming in the pool
Summertime is so cool

Steaks sizzling on the grill
Let's eat 'til we get our fill

I have absolutely no doubt
There is nothing better than a cookout

October 17, 2011

CRYING

Every once in a while I cry
Sometimes I don't even know why

A song I hear that reminds me of you
I am so grateful for a love that was so true

Sometimes I think of what I did wrong
That too, can be heard in a song

Sometimes I look at a cloud drifting by
I know that's a silly reason to cry

But, then again I do
I will shed a tear or two

Sometimes there is a smile behind the tear
I guess that's God's way of saying you're near

Sometimes I am ready to get up and go
And, something is hurting me so

I guess I will always have days that I am crying
But, there is no way I will ever be denying

How much I love you
And, I thank God for a love so true

December 26, 2011

DIFFICULT TIME OF THE YEAR

Christmas is really a rough time of the year
Even when those you love are near

When you have lost your mate
December 25th, is a difficult date

We try to smile as we send out the cards
But, it is so very hard

As we sit with friends and family
Opening gifts from under the tree

Watching loving couples kissing
Makes me realize what I am missing

The joy of Christmas Day
Left me when God took you away

EXPRESSIONS

Sometimes I look at the expressions on a person's face
I know some people wish they were in a different place

Some people take time to smile
They show a little class, a little style

Others look so sad
You wonder what happened to make life so bad

I always wish there was something I could do
So this person wouldn't feel so blue

Sometimes I try to just hold their hand
So they will know I want to understand

Some people look far away
They don't want to be here, but they stay

With some you can tell their mind is racing
And, amazingly, they aren't pacing

Some people stare off into outer space
There is no expression on their face

And, with some people, you know they care
Just by the smile with you they share

10/8/11

FALLING DOWN

Didn't you remember to turn on the light
When you got up in the middle of the night?

Did you fall down and bang your knee
When you got up to pee?

Did you think you were still in bed
When you fell down and hit your head?

Even though blue looks good on you
Black and blue just won't do

Even if it was a necessity
I am not sure I would get up to pee

Getting up in the middle of the night
Falling down and hitting your head isn't right

Because when you fall
911 is the number we call

You stub your toe
And, down you go

So even though the circus needs a clown
Stay in bed, DON'T fall down

March 19, 2012

FAMILY

A mother, father, and a child or two
Laughing, crying, fighting and loving, that's what families do

Moms, Dads sisters and brothers
Being there for one another

Having a meal and sharing your day
Listening to what each person has to say

A kiss and a hug to hold you tight
A shoulder to lean on when something is not right

A helping hand when you need a lift
Families are special if you get my drift

Through good times and bad
My family is the best anyone ever had

God created so many wonderful things
Flowers, trees, and birds that sing

But, families are the absolute best
And, I must say, I have been truly blessed

1/21/12

FRIENDS AGAIN

What a great way to spend the weekend!
Chatting with an old friend

Together we went to school
We didn't break too many rules

Then I married and you went away
I never got the opportunity to say

That I hoped we would always be friends
Then, several emails you did send

Suddenly, the phone rang and I knew
That once again I could talk to you

The memories after all these years
Brought smiles as well as tears

I know we can't erase yesterday
I know we'll be friends, come what may

You were my friend way back when
And, I am thrilled to say we are friends again.

August 17, 2010

HAPPY BIRTHDAY

I know it is true
I didn't give birth to you

I never held your hand when you were small
I never kissed your cut should you fall

I never bounced you on my knee
Or helped you catch butterflies only to set them free

And, even though I wasn't there in the beginning
All these years, my heart you've been winning

Now your birthday is near
I want to stand and cheer

You've become my daughter and my friend
Today, I want to send all the love I can possibly send

I wish you Happy Birthday
And, pray only good things come your way

May 26, 2011

HAPPY SPRING

My neighbor wished me a good day
Then I saw a chipmunk who had come out to play

Yards are being groomed
Flowers have started to bloom

You know it's spring
When, early in the morning, birds sing

Because the sun feels warm on my face
I walk at a slower pace

The gentle wind blows
And, the fragence of flowers hit my nose

Winter seemed to be hard and long
It left a lot of people sad and forlorn

But, at last, spring has arrived
And, I am so glad to be alive

11/8/11

HE NEVER SAID GOODBYE

I had hoped his love for me was strong
But; looking back, I was wrong

He said love was complicated
But, still he waited

He didn't wake me to say goodbye
He knew he would make me cry

I guess he loved me in his own way
Although I can't figure him out even today

He wanted love on his term
His committment wasn't firm

He was a coward, he couldn't watch me cry
So he left in the middle of the night and never said goodbye

9/14/12

HE STILL CALLS ME MOMMY

He can be very funny
He makes my day sunny

My little boy
Has always brought me great joy

He grew to be big and strong
He's the first to correct a wrong

He was quite a little lad
And, seldom was bad

I love it, and in a way, it's funny
But, at 41, he still calls me Mommy

4/28/12

HE WAS PLAYING A GAME

It’s amazing what one person can do
To make another happy or blue

A smile and a kiss
Can bring such bliss

Then one word said
Fills your heart with dread

One day you can’t stop smiling
The next you can’t stop crying

You know you’ll never feel the same
When you realize it was just a game

2/12/12

HEAVEN'S GLASS FLOOR

All of the loved ones who have gone before
Can see us through Heaven's glass floor

They can watch us and see what we do
No matter what, they still love me and you

Their love is unconditional and pure
On the other side of the glass floor

They give us a helping hand
By a way we don't understand

With the millions of souls up there
Watching us and somehow showing they still care

I wonder how long it will take
Before the glass floor will crack and break

But, like God's undying love, it will endure
Because it's Heaven's glass floor

7/14/12

HEY YOU

Hey You is a pretty shade of blue
He swims around because that's all he can do

If I tap on the glass
He swims over to me in a flash

His feelings have been ignited
You can tell he is excited

He's tiny and a pretty shade of blue
A cute little fish named Hey You

9/4/11

HURRICANE IRENE

I sit here at night
By the flickering candle light

The power has been out for more than a day and a half
So I make noises or try to laugh

The silence is so profound
The ticking of the clock is the only sound

Irene blew in with such force
Everyone was hoping she would be way off course

Granted she was not so strong
Thank God some of the forecasters were wrong

But, still after 24 hours
Sitting in the house with no power

Can be unsettleling that's true
I wonder what some folks will do

Food and milk will be spoiled
Our spirits dampened but not soiled

I guess trials like this bring back our pioneer spirit
But, I wish I had a radio with batteries so I could hear it

October 28, 2011

I APPRECIATE YOU

I am so glad we have become friends
I know on you I can depend

When I am sickly
You are here quickly

I love your friendly hello
And, the wave you give as you go

You have been so kind to me
I thank you for your sincerity

There are so many nice things you do
I just wanted to say how much I appreciate you

4/22/12

I LOVE THE MUSIC

The music was playing
And, my body was swaying

They were strumming the banjo
I sang all the songs I know

My feet were tapping on the floor
I love the music and wanted more

A man was singing like Louie Armsrtong
Listening to music like that, you can't go wrong

Clapping hands in time with the band
The music was just grand

It was a terrific way to end the day
Listening to great musicans play

I LOVE YOU MORE

As he started to walk through the door
He said "Honey, I love you more

I love you more than there are stars at night
I love you and want to hold you tight

I love hearing your voice
Loving you is the right choice

I love holding you near
And, calling you Honey Babe or Dear

In my arms is where you belong
You make my heart and love so strong

Because I treasure you
I want to bring pleasure to you

Honey, it is you I adore
And, I will always love you more"

6/13/12

I MUST BE BRAVE

Some people grow old gracefully
You know that won't be me

My crocheting has to be put away
My fingers are bending the wrong way

Walking is no longer a breeze
Even though I have 2 new knees

If I can get into the tub to take a bath
Getting out will really be a laugh

There's not one spot on my body that doesn't ache
Should I fall, I'm sure something will break

My hair was red
When I went to bed

But, someone snuck in during the night
And, changed the color to white

I must truly be brave
Because I am not ready for the grave

I PRETEND

I pretend you're here with me
I pretend our love will go on for eternity

I pretend our love is still true
I pretend it is still me and you

I pretend you're still holding me tight
I pretend you're still loving me through the night

I pretend I am fine
I pretend you'll always be mine

Sometimes pretending can be fun
But, when my time on earth is done

I hope God doesn't say this is not the end
I just wanted to pretend

You must go back and make amends
So next time, I won't have to say I pretend

I WENT TO CHURCH TODAY

I went to church today
God didn't say "I thought you ran away"

I didn't know if I could pray
God said it was o.k.

I know I haven't always been good
Or done all that I should

But, He opened His arms to me
And said " I love you unconditionally"

As I sat in that pew
I felt His love for me and you

I don't know what tomorrow will bring
Maybe I will hear angels sing

But, I went to church today
And, heard what God had to say

June 6, 2012

I WILL GET OVER YOU

You play games with a person's heart
I think I knew from the start

But, you weaved a web of deceit
For you, I gather a normal feat

You told me lie after lie
Many times you made me cry

I think of you when I am awake or asleep
I didn't realize my love for you was so deep

Your memory is still there
Even though I try not to care

The day will come and I will say
I was able to throw your memory away

Right now your memory makes me blue
But, I will get over you

2/29/12

I WONDER

I wonder what would happen to me
If I am not here for people to see

Is Heaven's streets lined with gold?
Do people stay young and never grow old?

Does everyone go through Heaven's doorway?
Is it always a beautiful day?

Will the people I've known, still remember me?
Will they be as they use to be?

Are there people, who instead, go to hell?
Does Satan ring his bell?

For all the lost souls
Does he make them pay a toll?

I prefer to think we are all Heaven bound
All the ones we have known and loved are waiting to be found

On the other side of Heaven's gate
They wait

7/16/12

I WOULDN'T DARE

We went for an ice cream treat
We ate inside to beat the heat

Three young girls came in
They made every man grin

The girls shorts were very tight and small
There was not a lot of material at all

God help them if they should sneeze
Their pants would have blown away from the breeze

If I were there age, I wouldn't dare to wear
Clothes so tight someone might wonder if I had on
underware

IF WE MET A LONG TIME AGO

If we met a long time ago,
Would I love you so?

If you asked me to marry, would I say I will?
I am sure it would have given me a tremendous thrill

Would I excite you the way you do me?
And, you do obviously

Would you put your arms around me
To hold me close as close as can be?

If we met a long time ago
Would you keep me close and never let go?

Would you walk with me side by side
Or ask me to be your bride?

I guess it's an answer we will never know
Because we never met a long time ago

4/28/12

IT HAPPENED AGAIN

It happened again last night
You called but I knew things weren't right

I know I probably shouldn't worry
But, you were in such a hurry

I didn't like the way you made me feel
Knowing you, you'll say Honey, it's no big deal

You have no clue
That you make me blue

I've known for a long time
You'll never be completely mine

I don't know what else to say
So I think I will just stay away

2/29/12

IT TAKES TIME

It takes time for things to grow
It takes time to learn things and to know

It takes time to learn to walk
It takes time to learn to talk

It takes time to learn to sing a song
It takes time to learn right from wrong

It takes time to learn to love
To put someone else above

It takes time to chase your dream
To learn to be part of the team

Things don't happen over night
It takes time, to make things right

IT'S ONLY POLITE

If you said you were going out
I would know what to tell people no doubt

If you said I will be gone for a day or two
I could tell people I am sorry, could someone else help you?

Or if I have a very important call to make
Please let them know I'll help if they can wait

It's nice to be polite
To try and make things right

Believe me, it's not too bold
To ask of things you should have been told

But, it just doesn't seem to work that way
There's a lot of inconsiderate people here, I must say

We were all taught manners a long time ago
Whatever happened to them, I would like to know

March 21, 2012

IT'S OVER

Your emails came through
I realized I had fallen for you

I looked for them every day
You made me laugh with what you'd say

I saved the emails so I could smile again
Then you suddenly stopped sending them

I kept hoping you'd miss me too
At least, half as much as I missed you

I reread the emails one by one
Tears filled my eyes when I was done

You had become very special to me
I hoped you would be more than a fantacy

But, today was the day
I got brave and through them away

JOHN AND BARRY

The love between father and son

When I first found out I was pregnant with you
I admit I was upset and not quite sure what to do

John took me to lunch
And, said he had had a hunch

I would be lying
If I said I wasn't crying

He held me close to him
And, gave me a loving grin

This child inside of me
Was definitly meant to be

The little seed began to grow
And, became the fine young man we both love so

You're father is the one
That made you the man you have become

He's the one with so much pride
And, a love from deep inside

He's the one that loves you so
More than you could ever know

It is because of the love he and I had
That we have you and we are so glad

He is the one that taught you to be a man
And, helped you to do the best you can

Dad loved you with all his heart
You will never be far apart

Dad will never be gone
Through you and your girls, he lives on

I know that at times, things get rough
But, you're just like him - loving and tough

You are the best part of your Dad and me
He will always be with you, you'll see

Sometime when you're feeling blue
Just remember how much we both love you

KIDS

Some kids still say “please” and “thank you”
Or ask if there is something they can do

Most kids are good as gold
And, do as they are told

Kids bring happiness when they come through the door
And, sometimes you wish you had more

When they look at you with an innocent face
It makes your heart race

Correct them when you must
But, don’t make such a big fuss

You are their Mom and Dad
Give them the love and guidance you had

They are small for such a short time
Hold them, love them, teach them a rhyme

Kids sometimes need to be corrected
And, always, always need to be protected

They are the world’s tomorrow
Don’t make their todays full of sorrow

Children are God’s gift to you
It’s up to you to show them what to do

9/30/11

KIND WORDS

When you choose to be kind
You never know what you'll find

For the most part
When you give from the heart

Blessings will come back to you
Thanking you for all you do

Shake someone's hand
Try to understand

Along with the handshake, give a smile
Make someone's day worthwhile

A smile and a kind word said
Can take away a person's fear and dread

It's amazing what one person can do
When they say "Hi, how are you?"

God says to be kinder than kind
You will be pleased with the rewards you find

LOST LOVE

At different times in my life
I loved someone enough to wish I were his wife

I lost my one true love, John
And, for him, I will always mourn

Then I found someone who made me smile
And, once again, life felt worthwhile

But, when we had to part
The pain broke my heart

It has become difficult to sleep
I wonder how long I will weep

It seems our love was not meant to be
Mourning is again a part of me

The pain cuts me to my very core
I think it's better for me, to love no more

October 22, 201

LOVE ACROSS THE MILES

You reached across the miles
Gave me love, gave me smiles

You always know what to say and do
You make me want more of you

I love it when you call me dear
And, I really want you near

But, since you've moved into my heart
I hate the miles that keep us apart

The time difference doesn't help much
Especially when I want and need your touch

But, I need you to know
That I do love you so

So even if time and miles keep us apart
You will always live in my heart

LOVE'S GLOW

The nursing home called and said don't worry
They called again and said please hurry

I waited outside for the girls to get here
But, the roads were bad and I had this fear

It seemed as though it took forever
I thought the snow would stop never

As I waited for the girls to arrive
Suddenly, I realized you were no longer alive

A warm yellow glow surrounded me
I could feel your love so gloriously

You had come to say goodbye
The warmth of your love filled the cold night sky

And, even now as I shed another tear
I can still feel your arms holding me

LUCKY ME

I thought I felt you touch my hair
When I looked around, you weren't there

Another time, you sat on my bed
And, I heard words you never said

I felt your warm touch
I realized I was loved so much

You have always been the best part of my life
I truly loved being your wife

You taught me the ways of love
Even now as you look down on me from up above

Not a day goes by that I don't think of you
How lucky I was to know a love so true.

MANY A DAY

It has been many a day since I thought and sat
It's been many a day since I wrote of this or that

Days seems to have flown by
I didn't write and don't know why

I guess other thoughts were in my head
Or I was just too tired when I went to bed

Some songs and memories would ring a bell
A poem about these would really be swell

I couldn't even say things will be all right
My mind seemed to be shut down tight

Now it is springtime once more
Hopefully writing will no longer be a chore

I guess there are times we all need a break
So I think I'll have a cup of tea and a piece of cake.

April 1, 2011

MOTHER NATURE'S CRUEL JOKE

What happened to the sunshine
Or writng, in the sand, "be mine"

Or the long walk on a spring day
Or just sitting on a park bench to pass the time away

Everyday seeing the flowers grow
It's April first, and they are under a foot of snow

April Fool's Day what a joke
Had to buy oil and went broke

Snow, sleet, and rain
Mother Nature can be a pain

1/27/12

MOTHERS

I don't think parents are parents any more
I saw two mothers, one coming in and the other going out the door

The mothers walked with one child and not the other
It was as if the last child was a bother

The boy was about 5, the girl about 3
And, the mothers were just too busy

I get so angry when I see something like this
I wish these little kids were mine, that's my wish

I would give them love and hold their hands
I would try to be the best mother in the land

What makes a mother let her child walk behind?
I see this so often it blows my mind

A child is so precious, so small
Hold their hand so they don't fall

Parents are suppose to protect and love their little ones
And, tuck them safely into bed when the day is done

5/9/11

MOTHER'S DAY

It was Mother's Day
And, my girls took me back to yesterday

We went back to where I use to live
Such a thoughtful gift for my girls to give

On Friend Court, where I married and changed my name
All of the houses were no longer the same

Then up to where my parents had moved to
It was a very thoughtful thing for my girls to do

We roamed all around
Wonderful memories were found

So many homes up for sale
But, the memories were there without fail

Then we drove around some more
Up near the ocean on the Northshore

We found a nice place to eat
Such a delightful treat

It was such a wonderful way
To spend Mother's Day

MY BEST FRIEND

God said I think I will send
Pamela to be your best friend

She will laugh with you
And, cry with you too

She will give you moral support
And, be a great cohort

Pamela will share stories with you
And, always have a smile or two

She will tease you in a friendly way
You will know, with Pamela, when things are ok

I'm giving Pamela a special place in your heart
Forever you'll be friends as you were from the start

You may not be as tall as she
But, a better friend, you will never see

5/21/12

MY CHILD

You are my moonbeam on the darkest night
You're my ray of sunshine when it's light

You're my pot of gold at the end of a rainbow
You are all the good things the world should know

You're my warmth on a cold winter's day
You are the one I thank God for, what more can I say?

You are the reason I smile
You definitly make my life worthwhile

Dec.2.2011

MY DAUGHTER AND I

It suddenly dawned on me
That my daughter has become the mother I use to be

When she was small and having fun
I was trying to get things done

If she was sickly
I'd try to make her well quickly

But, now she takes care of me
Doing everything that is necessary

Now she makes me a meal
And, asks how I feel

Or she says "Do you need anything at the store?
Don't worry, Mom, I will wash the floor"

Mom, I know you always did your best
Now it is time for you to sit and rest.

I love you, Mom

6/17/12

MY FANTACY

On an island is where I would like to be
Just you and me and the beautiful blue sea

Walking on the beach
The ocean within reach

The warm sand between my toes
The smell of the salt water touching my nose

The palm trees
Gently swaying in the breeze

There is a shelter from a storm
And, two arms to keep me warm

I know this is just a fantacy
But, it sure sounds good to me

MY FAVORITE CHAIR

When the arthritis hurts because it is going to rain
And, I am feeling a lot of pain

I get comfy in my big chair
Maybe even hug my teddy bear

My chair and a nice cup of tea
Bring a lot of comfort to me

I can rest my weary bones
Even if I am not alone

If the day seems to be dreary
And, my body feels weary

I don't even have to count sheep
I sit in my favorite chair and fall asleep

August 21, 2011

NO CLUE

I know you don't have a clue
That sometimes you make me feel blue

Sometimes I just don't know
How you can say you love me so

When I say something to you
You have no understanding, no clue

You think it is ok
Just to say

Honey, I love you
And, that's all you need to do

But, actions speak louder than words
It's things not said that I heard

So many times you make me feel blue
Unfortunately, you have no clue

December 18,2011

ONCE AGAIN

Had I listened at the start
I would not have a broken heart

I really believed the words you said
Now each day, I wake up with dread

When you called the other night
I knew something wasn't right

In the background, I heard a voice
And, I knew, I had no other choice

Your wife or your friend, I will never know
And, I realize I have to let you go

Once again, you made me cry
Once again, I thought I would die

7/22/11

ONE NATION UNDER GOD

When I was in school
We learned the Golden Rule

We put our hands over our hearts to salute the flag
Now, to some, it means nothing, it's a drag

We would bow our heads and say
The Lord's Prayer every day

If, for some reason, a student's family said it wasn't allowed
It was ok. We are Americans and we stood proud

It did not matter, a person's race
Nor did the person's color or faith

Together, in that classroom, we were one
Now, all we were taught, is coming undone

There were proper things to do
We were proud of our red, white and blue

We were young, old, white and black
Now, God help us, we're under attack

I am proud to be an American
Together we can stand

And, it should be gratifying, not odd
That we are ONE NATION UNDER GOD

OUR AMERICAN FLAG

Our American flag flying in the breeze
I am in awe of the feeling it leaves

The stripes and stars
Have led us so far

It's time we, once again, stood proud
And, to let our united voices shout out loud

Give us back the pride we once knew
As well as the promises made for me and you

Our forefathers thought of our future
That we, as a nation, should continue to nurture

We can no longer take our freedom for granted
When other counties' views of us have become so slanted

2/29/12

PRICE INCREASE

The price of gas went up again
The increases have to stop, but when?

People need to buy food and can't
Some people just rave and rant

But, nothing is being done it seems
And, the cost of living is too extreme

Government officials don't seem to care
They get paid and aren't on welfare

They don't have to pay for medical bills
They sit in their office on Federal Hill

If we re-elect them they say
We will no longer have to pay and pay

They promise the cost of things will come down
I think most of them are a bunch of clowns

I use to respect our government
But, it's time for the politicians to repent

America use to be respected
Now our country is rejected

The officials need to stop being so greedy
And, to help America's needy

June 30, 2011

RED LIGHT

I looked into the mirror and saw her face
There was no look of happines, not a trace

We were stopped at a red light, but she wanted to go
Then she passed me and I wasn't going very slow

We had another red light
On her face, I saw fright

What a way to start the day
But, she hit evey red light on the way

She had her cell phone in her hand
Guess she was trying to make someone understand

She was definitly going to be late
But, she hit every red light and had to wait

June 7, 2011

SECRETS

I love you too much to let you go
But, there is so much about you I don't know

So many things you don't want to share
Even though I am sure you care

I don't want to be just a toy
I want to give you love and joy

You've turned my heart upside down
And, I want you to always be around

The way you love me
So warm and tenderly

But, yet I fear
You won't always be near

All the secrets you keep from me
Make me wonder about your sincerity

I believe you when you say "I love you"
I pray those words will always be true

All the secrets that you keep
I hope won't, someday, make me weep

9/10/11

SHE FELL AND I CRIED

I saw something today
It made me cry and pray

In a very busy market place
A lady fell down on her face

All I could think of was you
You would fall and there was nothing I could do

I cried all the way home
Made a call and cried on the phone

Then, tonight, when I should have been in bed
I cried my heart out instead

All the times you fell
I remember them so well

Most days I am mostly ok
Then I see something like I saw today

Uncontrollable tears fall from my eyes
I continue to cry and then sigh

I know there was nothing I could do
But, seeing this poor lady reminded me of you

10/29/11

SHE WAS 10

She had numbers tattooed on her arm
Someone caused her a lot of harm

I didn't know what to say or do
She was 10, like me and you

My eyes seem to linger
On her hand with a missing finger

She was quiet and shy
Sometimes she would cry

When I asked what was wrong, she wouldn't say
I realize now, bad memories got in the way

She said she would rather lose a finger than die
I hugged her and we both started to cry

I don't know what happened way back then
But, she was my friend and she was only 10

SOMEONE NEW

Someone opened the door and you came in
With your warm eyes and sexy grin

There was a cockiness about you
And, my head said he's too good to be true

I tried to pretend I didn't care
But, every day I looked for you everywhere

Day by day my feeings grew stronger
Until I could not hold back a moment longer

Now I find I want to be close to you
Wishing it was just we two

SQUIRREL AT THE FEEDER

I watched the squirrel climb the tree
He thought "This bird food looks good to me

I can get some on the ground
Because it is scattered all around

There is more hanging up there
I'm pretty sure the birds want to share

If I walk out on the branch very slow
They wouldn't even know

I am going to get lots of seed
Because their food is what I need"

9/2/2010

THE SQUIRREL VS THE PT CRUSIER

Caught in the headlights of an on coming car
The little squirrel is mushed into the tar

He thought you were playing a game
When suddenly he realized, you had taken aim

He brought his little paws up as if to pray
And, said "Oh heck, this is the end of my day"

The poor little thing had a tear in his eye
When he bent over to kiss his ass goodbye

But, if by chance, he didn't die
You better watch out when you go whizzing by

He has the number of your pt cruiser
And, man, are you going to be a loser

He is going to call his friends over to visit you
Just wait and see what some well planted acorns can do

TALKING TO GOD

You're a friend and I could ask you
What do you think I should do?

But, there are times I have to ask why
A precious child had to die

There are times I feel so alone
I sit and wait by the telephone

But, nothing happens, it doesn't ring
I will turn on my music and pretend I can sing

Most times I have a smile on my face
I know I am in the right place

So if I am down and feeling blue
Dear God, I know I can talk to you

I know you are always near
Whether I am smiling or have a tear

I know your hand is holding mine
Helping me to walk the line

All these things I know are true
But, Dear God, there are days I am blue

I try to hold my head up high
Although there are times I need to cry

I ask to have a good day
You make the sun shine along my way

At night when I go to bed
I thank you for taking me on the path you led

I may not do everything right
But, I pray to you every night

I may not always know what to do
But, Dear God, I know I can always talk to you

TEN CENT MOVIES

Shopping has become such a chore
Buying less and spending so much more

I don't know what I would do
If I had children to feed too

I remember having fifty cents in my hand
I thought that was just grand

I could go to the movies for a dime
My friends and I had a great time

We had enough money for popcorn and penny candy too
What a great treat for me and you

For a nickle, we could buy a big frosty root beer
It was so good, we would always cheer

Now, we have to get a loan
Or refinace our home

Just to be able to do
All the things we use to

2/2/12

TEXTING

Years ago, people never had a cell phone
They used a phone in the office or at home

But, things have drastically changed
Our lives have been totally rearranged

Cell phones are now smaller and "better"
You can talk or even send a letter

If you go out to dine
What do you find?

Mothers, fathers and kids too
Texting as if they had nothing better to do

Just because I find it quite rude
Some people think I have an attitude

Driving and texting is not a smart thing to do
You're apt to kill a person or two

Believe me I am not paranoid
But, I really do get annoyed

Everyone everywhere is texting
I just find it totally perlexing

It would be nice, if for a little while
You stopped texting and gave someone a smile

8/2/10

THANK YOU

All the kind words you say
Make me happy that you came my way

All the things that you do
Make me so grateful for you

You help me up if I fall
You always remember to call

For all the things that you do
I am so thankful for you

THANK YOU U.S. MILITARY

They stand so straight and tall
These men and women who give their all

I was proud to shake their hands
To thank them for protecting our land

Although I am sorry they have to carry a gun
I am still proud of each and every one

The Army, Navy, Air Force, Coast Guard and Marines
Are the most dedicated people I have ever seen

To be able to thank you, our country's treasure
Truly gives me great pleasure

Because of you, our country is alive
And, without you, we could not survive

So I want to thank each and every one of you
For your sacrifices and all that you do

Because we all know it is true
Without you, there would be no red, white and blue

9/6/12

THE AFTERMATH

Trees and wires are down
It's dark all over town

Gilette Stadium had lights
But, for the seniors, daytime was like night

No emergency lights in the hall
Made me worry about the seniors having a fall

Wires lie across the street
You really have to watch where you put your feet

There are sick and needy all over the town
Everywhere you looked, trees and wires were down

But, Gillette Stadium had lights
Because the Patriots were playing on Thursday night

God bless the police and fire department
They were here, they are the angels God sent

They checked on everyone here
They helped us if we had fear

The Patriots had power
But our police and fire department, are the men of the hour

December 29, 2010

THE BEST GIFT OF ALL

The best gift of all
Isn't a bike or a bouncing ball

It isn't a new car
Or a trip that takes you far

It's a loving smile from a friend
A hand to hold until the end

A shoulder to cry on if you need to
A person that says I'm here for you

A tear and a smile when a baby is born
The bright sunshine in the early morn

The stars that sparkle in the sky
The way a friend smiles when they say hi

All these, as nice as they are
It is not the answer you desire

The best gift of all is from above
That is the gift of love, unconditional love

THE CHICK CLIQUE

Budda bing, budda bang
This is the chick gang

Cathy is the chick
In charge of the clique

Along with seven other ladies and me
We are the best bunch of chicks you'll ever see

At our age, we've seen a lot of grief
But, we are able to laugh, and that's a relief

We get together and have lots of fun
And, there is never any harm done

So if you see a crowd
Don't be surprised to hear us laugh out loud

We are beautiful chicks
And, this is our clique

THE GAME

I should have listened to my heart
When it said "Don't Start

But, you said words I needed to hear
Words that made me want you near

But, like the cards we play
It's a game to you, what more can I say?

Some day I hope I learn
Not to tell anyone how I yearn

To you, I am nothing more than a toy
You're not looking for real joy

I'm better off putting my heart back on the shelf
And, play solitaire by myself

June 9, 2011

THE LIGHTS WENT OUT

When will the lights come back on, I don't know
But, I have the candles all aglow

We're in the midst of a thunderstorm
That seems to go on and on and on

I found a light I forgot I had
Now, I can see and it's not so bad

Tomorrow I will stock up on batteries
Lots of C's and D's

I will get extra candles to spread around
And, definitly say a prayer to keep me safe and sound

There's an alarm that keeps on beeping
Hope it doesn't keep me from sleeping

It's still raining, I can hear it pour
And, the lights have been out for an hour or more

I have nothing better to do
So I will sit here and think of you

7/25/12

THE MADMAN

For absolutely no reason
A madman did an act of treason

People go to a movie for fun
And, this madman takes out a gun

For reasons we will probably never know
Our American Flag, once again, flies low

He did not care if the victims were young or old
He'll probably say, he heard voices and did as he was told

Over the past several years
America has shed too many tears

This animal took children, husband and wives
And, he ruined so many lives

I know we are taught not to hate
But, I pray St. Peter doesn't let him through the Pearly Gate

He will never be sorry nor will he repent
I pray to God, Hell is where he is sent

2/9/12

THE OLD ROCKING CHAIRS

On the porch, are two old rocking chairs
My Daddy and I would sit there

Sometimes we would try to count the stars
Or even catch fire flies in a jar

Sometimes we would just sit and talk.
Or once in a a while go for a walk

Then he would race me to my favorite chair
It was great when he was there

If I was scared, he would comfort me
He would hold on his lap, and rock me gently

It's too bad fathers and their kids don't do that any more
It's important, it's fun, and should not be a chore

If I had a porch and two old rocking chairs
On a summer's night, you and I could sit there

5/19/12
For Kaitlen Maclean

THE PENDANT

It seems like yesterday you sat on my knee
Today, you're a bride and so pretty

This was the ring your Dad gave to me
Pledging his love for all eternity

We had it made into a pendant just for you
To wear on the day you say "I do"

As you and Dan stand side by side
Our hearts are full of love and pride

6/6/12

THE POOR LITTLE BIRD

The poor little bird was confused
His way he did lose

Robin Red Breast knocked on your door
Unfortunately he left a little poop on the porch floor

He doesn't mean to alarm you
And, certainly would never harm you

The poor bird has come to you for 3 years now
What a tribute to you-----WOW

He wants you to know
He really loves you so

The Poor little bird
All he could give, was a little turd

November 30, 2010

THE SACRED NIGHT

Christmas lights that shine so bright
Like the star on that Sacred night

As all the bells are ringing
You can almost hear the angels singing

After all these years that have past
God still gives us a love that will forever last

A love so steadfast and true
A love just for me and you

We can feel His embrace
Even as we look upon His face

There can be peace within us all
If we try to answer His call

Thousands of years have flown by
Since that star shown in the night's sky

And, all these beautiful Christmas lights
Still remind us of that long ago Sacred night

5/3/12

THE TIRE SWING

I saw a tire swing hanging from a tree
What memories it brought back to me

We didn't have swing sets like kids do today
But we really had fun when we went out to play

Playing hop scotch and jumping rope
We would toss a ball, and we always had hope

Even in the rain, we'd find something to do
Maybe look for bugs or a frog or two

Of course, we'd make mud pies
And, be covered in mud from our toes to our eyes

On the tire swing, we could go to the moon and back
Or pretend it was a train going down the track

We could swing high or swing low
Make it go fast or slow

We could twist it in circles and have a ball
We would get dizzy when got off and fall

The tire swing was so much fun
Makes me wish I still had one

THINKING OF YOU

At night when I am in my bed
Thoughts of you go through my head

I always seem to want you near
But, that will never happen I fear

As I close my eyes and try to sleep
Through my head you seem to creep

You have no idea how I wish you could hold me
To kiss me and love me tenderly

Some nights I toss around for hours
I long to call you, but I cower

My love for you seems to grow
Why this is, I honestly don't know

Now it's late and I need to sleep
But, thoughts of you into my head will creep

TIME GETS AWAY

Time gets away
I will do it another day

I am so busy right now
Will I get things done? I wonder how

So many things I must do
I don't have time for me or you

When I go to bed
So many thoughts rush through my head

So many challenges I have to face
Means too many memories I will have to erase

The children have grown much to fast
Why didn't their childhood last?

Unfortunately everyone I know is the same boat
I pray to God, together, we can stay afloat

March 7, 2012

WHAT HAPPENED TO TRADITIONS?

Holidays aren't the same anymore
They have become an expensive chore

People have to work a job or two
Then rush home with much more to do

They run helter skelter every where
I can't say don't rush - I don't dare

I still care, I really do
But, their attitudes make me blue

Some people do more than their share
While others relax in an easy chair

It's nice that some family traditions have been passed on
Unfortunately, so many more are gone

06/11/11

WAITING FOR YOUR CALL

Another night and you keep me waiting
Is this your idea of dating?

I sit here all alone
Waiting for you to phone

It seems as if hours go by
I promised myself I would not cry

Do you think I am joking?
Am I just a love token?

Do you say you love me to make it right?
To me, it is just another sleepless night

Sometimes I can't believe how much I hurt
And, yet I let you make me feel like a jerk

But, I guess this will have to do
Until I can find someone who's love is true

WHEN I WAS SMALL

A long time ago when I was small
There was no shopping on Sundays at all
Matter of fact, we didn't even have a mall

Television was relatively new
The kids still had plenty to do
We'd be outside playing, just me and you

Families would go for a long ride
Off to the beach and watch the tide
Our friends would try to find us when we would hide

We would go for a ride on our bikes
Sometimes we would take a hike
It was you, Johnny and oh yes Mike

Our families would gather from here and there
There would be so many, we would need an extra chair
Games would be played fair and square

Sunday school and church were a priority
You knew your neighbors or at least the majority
There seemed to be more peace and tranquility

We went to church, we went to school
We learned to live by the Golden Rule
Our way of life was simple, but oh so cool

THINKING OF YOU WHEN YOU LOST SOMEONE

I am sitting here thinking of you
Knowing all you are going through

I know there is nothing I can do or say
To take your pain away

I know your heart
Feels as if it has been torn apart

We both know that is true
And, you wonder what you'll do

You'll scream and cry
Always asking why

It will take a while
But, one day you will smile

It won't happen overnight
But, the day will come and you wil be alright

In the meantime, if you need a hug, I'm here for you
Or to shed some tears, we can do that too

LOSING FRIENDS

One by one I watch them go
Going up to Heaven to be with God you know

Friends, I have lost so many
Before long I won't have any

It is devastaing to see
I wonder why not me?

Why am I still here?
Is death far away or near?

I am assuming God has a plan for me
I have no idea what it should be

Hopefully, one day it will be clear
While everyone else is gone and I'm still here

I will do my best to carry on
Until God shows me the great beyond

MY ANGEL, JOHN

You hold my hand and I hold yours
Together we can open all the doors

There is absolutely nothing we can't do
The two of us; me and you

I will be with you every step of the way
While you're working or at play

I will be with you day and night
Loving you, guiding you and holding you tight

You may not always see me there,
But, in your heart, you'll know I will always care

You will never be alone
I am your love, your very own.

BEAU

Move over, Beau is coming through
He wants to say hello to you

Beau is such a lovable dog
A beacon of light in the thickest fog

He is such a joy
Bringing pleasure wherever he goes

He looks as if he has a smile on his face
When he beats Ann in a race

Ann would say no
Beau would look at her as if to say watch me go

He would run as fast as he could
Sometimes to the bench or to the woods

I think a dog is God's way
To make you smile everyday

7/9/2011

BETTY

When I did something dumb, who did I call? Betty
Who was always ready to laugh at it all? Betty

Who would try to call me on the tv remote? Betty
Who would laugh at me before I finished a joke? Betty

Who encouraged me to write? Betty
Who would say you're probably right? Betty

Who would say I remember a 100 years ago? Betty
Who was the woman Mom and Dad loved so? Betty

If I did something silly, she said
Oh I must remember to tell Fred

Who was a tremendous part of my life? Betty
I'm so glad Norm chose you for a wife, Betty

I love you and will miss you
So call if you have a mind to

10/06/43 to 02/04/03

BILLY

We buried Billy today
He was much to sick to stay

He made us laugh and sometime cry
Fifty nine is too young to die

Billy touched the heart of quite a few
Years ago, he touched mine too

God knew Billy was in pain
So He brought Billy to heaven on his very own train

BILL SHEEHAN

We buried Bill today
He was much to sick to stay

His complexion was so pale
And, he had become so frail

Bill was my neighbor, my friend
He was a gentle man to the very end

Bill was a kind man in every sense of the word
I know our prayers for him were heard

Bill, God knew you were in a great deal of pain
He's bringing you home in your own heavenly train.

CAROL DOBSON

When you find someone you truly love
The time you have together is never enough

I am so glad Carol came into your lilfe
And, so happy you made her your wife

By doing that you gave us a new family member
One, we will always love and remember

I know over the years, she gave so much love to you
She will always be with you, no matter what you do

When people we love leave
We will forever grieve

But, I do believe we will see them again
It might be in a moon beam or a drop of rain

One way or another, they let us know they are there
They want us to know they still care

Carol will forever remain in our hearts
As she did from the very start

7/26/12

THE BRIGHTEST STAR

for
Dottie Lindberg

I have been trying to think of a word or two
To say about you

You were a warm and gentle person
And, I know you were a lot of fun

Today we have to say goodbye
To a wonderful lady who tried

She was a true and loyal friend
From the beginning to the end

She said one day, she had forgotten how to pray
I told her God heard every word she had to say

She had no way of knowing
All the love she was showing

She was always in the mood
For chocolate and pepsi, her favorite food

Tonight I will look for the brightest star
That way I will know exactly where you are

7/25/12

CAROL AND DOTTIE

Today I lost a sister and a friend
Two different people united in the end

Cancer took them both away
Same month, same day

I am so grateful they were here
These two people I will forever hold dear

In many ways they were alike
But, different as day and night

I was so afraid to say goodbye
Oh Lord, I didn't want them to die

I guess I am being greedy
And, probably very needy

They were so sick
I am really grateful it was quick

But, I still have to ask why
These wonderful people had to die

03/15/11

CAROL JOHNSTON

Cancer has taken another life
It added more stress and strife

It's a horrible way to die
And, those left behind ask why

Family and friends try to be strong
And, praying to God is not wrong

Everyone had hoped and prayed she would recover
But, now two children are left without a mother

You feel their grief and their pain
And, wonder how to keep from going insane

It seems to me, there must be a cure
Because this is too much for any family to endure

CAROLYN'S BUTTERFLIES

Butterfly balloons are set free
Drifting across the sky aimlessly

We stood and watched them flying high
It was a beautiful way to say goodbye

When the balloons finally took flight
We all knew you were finally alright

I can't imagine all you went through
No matter what, your smile was always true

You thought of everyone else before yourself
Concern for yourself went on the back shelf

Your children and family meant the world to you
With all their hearts, they loved you too

Rainbows, angels and butterflies too
Special things that will always remind us of you.

1/15/11

CHRIS

Chris was a friend of mine
He was a ray of sunshine

A breathe of fresh air
Someone who would always care

Chris had a warm easy style
And, always, always had a smile

Chris was polite and kind
A treasure hard to find

He was a friend that you never want to let go
Chris was such a joy to know

Chris was awesome, gentle and kind
I thank God, he was a friend of mine

ERIN

How do we say goodbye
To someone too young to die?

Erin was so full of life
She was a good mom and a loving wife

Erin had an infectious smile
She made every minute of her life worthwhile

She had courage beyond belief
Erin would want us to smile even in our grief

Long ago the doctors said it was time for her to go
But, Erin said I'm not ready, oh no

I still have much to do and so far to go
And, my family, Oh God I love them so

Unfortunately, Erin no longer has the strength to fight
Dear God, she's earned her wings, please let her take flight

Bring her home to you
She has gone through more than anyone should go through

Dear Erin, it is time to say goodbye
To someone too young to die

ETHEL MAC FARLANE

She didn't say good bye
She didn't mean to make me cry

The weather was bad
Storm after storm we had

I will always see her curled up in her chair
I hope she knew that I really did care

She always had a warm smile
Ethel made my life worthwhile

I loved her from the very first day
Her friendship with me will always stay

Ethel was such a special friend
I'm so sorry I wasn't there for her at the end

Ethel, if you can hear me
I will always think of you tenderly

You were a special lady
And, I thank you for being a friend to me

GEORGE

He was my hero
I loved him so

He always had time for me
Made the me the biggest snowman for everyone to see

He had personality plus
And, boy could he cuss

His wit was keen
And, he had the bluest eyes I have ever seen

No one ever knew what George would do
He surprised my parents and shocked the neighbors too

But, George was my big brother
And, I loved him as no other

When the doctor said George wasn't going to live
I said I had lots of blood that I would give

I gave my blood and white cells too
The doctor wanted my bone marrow, George said please not you

I held his hand and tried not to cry
Oh Lord, I didn't want my brother to die

But, George wasn't ready to go

He loved us all I know

He survived for many years
Even now, I still shed tears

But, as I held his hand and tried not to weep
George closed his eyes and went to sleep

GERI

No matter how hard I try
It is so difficult to say good bye

You were such a special friend
Forgive me for not being there at the end

You would look off into space
Not recognizing anyone's face

"Granny" is what my John called you
But, in his heart, he loved you too

You made us smile
You had your own unique style

Now you are going home to God's place
And, there is a look of calmness on your face

But, no matter how hard I try
It's so difficult to say good bye

I love you, Geri

GINNY

God said, "Ginny, today is the day"
She said "Please, God, let me stay

I still have things to do
Let my children grow before I come home to you"

Everyday He watched her and would smile
He thought letting her stay was worthwhile

But, now there's no more for you to do
And, I need you too

So let's do this right
Just close your eyes and come to the light

George, Bobby, your parents, Jackie and Gerry
They need you now so please hurry

Ginny you always did your very best
It's time for your eternal rest

So my precious, Ginny, know in your heart
You've been loved from the very start

1-0 8-08

GORDON CLARK

Another day
Another friend passed away

We're left wondering why he had to die
At least, we had a chance to say goodbye

It's still so sad
We have to remember the good times we had

He always greeted us with a smile on his face
Now he'll smile from a better place

He was a warm and gentle man
He would always try to understand

Hopefully, all his pains will cease
And, he will find eternal peace

April 27, 2011

JUDY

He walks around in such dispair
Knowing she's gone and won't be there

His heart in his hand
Saying, God, I don't understand

She was my wife
The love of my life

When she died, part of me died too
Now I wonder what am I to do?

I go through the motions of everyday life
But, it's not the same without my wife

I know in my heart she is with you
And, she's not suffering, that's true

There are times I feel her near
Or I hear a sweet whisper in my ear

As I think of our lives together, I smile
Loving Judy made my life worthwhile

7/9/11

IN HER CHAIR

She closed her eyes, thought she would rest
Her hands were crossed upon her chest

She looked as if she didn't have a care
As she slept in her easy chair

But, she didn't move at all
When on the phone, I did call

I let the phone ring and ring
Suddenly, I heard an angel sing

As she slept, God let her have a last sigh
Then, brought her to His home on high

He was pleased in the person she had become
And, said "Betty, your time on earth is done.

From here you can see your family and friends
This is just the beginning, not the end."

MATTHEW

Whether it's sunny or if it should rain
My heart is empty, there is so much pain

I feel your smile when the sun shines so bright
I laugh when I think of looking for deer by starlight

A gentle breeze kisses my face
I know it's you from a better place

I know you are always near me
When I pray, I know you hear me

I laughed, you tried
You died, I cried

Every day I think of you
I will always love you, my Matthew

10/02/05

MAYNARD

God said Maynard, come it's time to rest
I know how hard you struggled, you did your best

You've been a loving husband, a good friend
Now it's time for your suffering to end

Come here and sit with me
I have a special fishing pole just for thee

From here you can see
All the fishes wherever they may be

So come now, it's time for rest
You are special and passed all the tests

MILLIE

What do you say
When another friend passes away?

You try to comfort those left behind
With words that are kind

But, their passing as left you blue
And, you are hurting too

The memories are there
And, sometimes it helps to share

Think back to yesterday
All the laughs we had on the way

Millie was loved by all
Then she had to answer God's call

So even though we miss her it's true
We're lucky because she loved us too

RAY BIRD

Maybe it's best for us not to know
How God plans for us to go

And, it's hard to know exactly what to say
When someone special passes away

A special bond between he and you
Ray was more than family, he was a friend too

Although, his passing has left you feeling sad
For the love, friendship and happiness he gave, be glad

It's easy for people to say don't cry
But, it is still hard when you have to say good bye

Ray was your cousin, your friend
So it is with love this poem I send

ROSE

Most people only have one mother
Rose and I have sort of adopted each other

She is one of the nicest people I know
And, I have come to love her so

We try to help each other get through the day
We hold hands along the way

I lend her a hand, she lends me two
Without her, sometimes I wonder what I would do

Rose is a lady and she is so nice
I have truly been blessed twice.

I love you, Rose.

December 21, 2010

THE CALL

She is a stranger in this place
Looking for a familiar face

This is a place she no longer wants to be
She is looking there, I wonder what does she see

To me it is just a wall
But, I think she is waiting for the call

As she stares off into space
There is still a look of beauty on her face

She is tired, there is no need to roam
She needs the angels to come take her home

It's time for Rose to go to sleep
To be with our Savior and His sheep

He is holding out His hand to you
Close your eyes and go, that's all you need to do

Because of you, we have all been blessed
Now, it's time for your eternal rest

6/3/11

TRIPOD

I don't think it is the least bit odd
That you would name your cat Tripod

A warm, fuzzy ball of fur
He snuggles up against you and purrs

He brought you joy and made you smile
You made his life worthwhile

Cats are as indepenent as can be
That's probably why he chose you, don't you agree?

I know he loved you so
But, Tripod was suffering and had to go

If cats have a heaven that's where he'll be
And, in your heart, he'll live on, you'll see